030

C000051206

POCKET GUIDE
MODERN
AIRLINERS

Richard Aboulafia & Renée Gentry

HarperCollins*Publishers*

In the UK for information address:
HarperCollins*Publishers*
77-85 Fulham Palace Road
Hammersmith
London W6 8JB

First Published in Great Britain by HarperCollins*Publishers* 1999

1 3 5 7 9 10 8 6 4 2

© HarperCollins*Publishers* 1999

ISBN 0 00 472228 0

Design: Rod Teasdale

Colour reproduction by Colorscan
Printed in Italy

POCKET GUIDE

MODERN AIRLINERS

Contents

Contents

Introduction

A Powerful Force For Change

Until very recently, there were three types of world travelers: soldiers, missionaries, and the very rich. The arrival of the modern commercial jetliner in the late 1950s transformed this situation. Boeing's 707, De Havilland's Comet, and Douglas's DC-8 made air travel affordable for the upper middle classes. The advent of the widebody aircraft, with Boeing's 747 in 1969, extended the franchise to the middle classes. US airline deregulation in the 1980s further decreased costs, making air travel affordable to the overwhelming majority of the public.

As a result, we live in a much smaller world. Every year, the percentage of people who have visited foreign cultures increases. Presumably, this helps cultures better understand each other, and hopefully diminishes the prospect of a major war. Meanwhile, low air cargo costs stimulate international trade, particularly time-urgent goods such as flowers or very high value electronics. In all, jetliners are a consistently positive force for global change.

Having said all of the above, manufacturers today face a major challenge: What to do next? The world has decided that the optimum airborne people-mover has thin wings with high-bypass podded turbofan engines. Most of the jetliners built today have their origins in the 1960s and 1970s. Engines have become incrementally more efficient, the cockpit has lost its third person, but there have been no 'show-stoppers'.

Supersonic designs have proven prohibitively expensive, as evidenced by the Concorde's market failure. Very high bypass engines (propfans) met customer resistance, and have been made redundant by low oil prices.

The world, in short, is running out of useful, revolutionary new commercial airliner technologies. Without major aircraft cost improvements, travel growth rates will slow. Another result of this technological plateau is that many of the aircraft featured in this book will remain in service for at least the next few decades. And many of the jetliners being produced today will remain in production for the foreseeable future. The first Boeing 747s, for example, were delivered in 1969, and the latest model, the 747-400, has orders extending past 2004. Boeing will also update the design, and the resulting 747-500 will almost certainly be in production past 2015.

The exception to this unexceptional state of affairs is the regional aircraft industry. The market for regional aircraft, used by smaller local carriers and regional subsidiaries of the major airlines, has been transformed by the arrival of the new generation regional jet.

Turboprop-powered aircraft, once the dominant component of this market, have been steadily pushed out by jets, and now comprise a mere 40% of the market by dollar value (in current year deliveries). The story began in the 1980s, with the arrival of numerous new prop designs. De Havilland Canada's Dash 8 series, ATR's 42/72, British Aerospace's Jetstream 31 and ATP, Fokker's F50, Saab's 340, and Embraer's 120 all entered service in this time. More prop designs, including Dornier's Do.328, Saab's 2000, and British Aerospace's Jetstream 41 entered service in the early 1990s.

The astonishing aspect of this era was that most of these programs were relatively successful. While ongoing market share wars kept profits low (or kept losses high), very large numbers of turboprop regional aircraft were delivered. Just to mention one segment, over 1,100 30-seat turboprops were delivered between 1986 and 1996. Yet even in this prop-dominated era, jets still impacted the market. British Aerospace's 146 (later reborn as the Avro RJ) was at one point marketed as a 'hub raider', for regional operations.

In the late 1980s, numerous manufacturers began design studies for regional aircraft powered by turbofans. Of the myriad proposals, the only ones to reach the market were low-cost derivatives of existing aircraft designs. The first new jet to reach the market was Bombardier/Canadair's CRJ. This design spent the late 1980s and early 1990s in limbo. In 1988, Canadair announced memoranda of understanding with several airlines covering 42 CRJs. This list of commitments was later increased to 150 planes. Most of these later evaporated, and when deliveries began in late 1992 there were only 36

orders. However, the initial users were extremely happy with the type, and orders soon arrived in considerable numbers. By October 1998, over 420 CRJ orders had been received.

The CRJ was followed by Fokker's F70, a 78-seat shrink of the 107-seat F100 jetliner. While a promising design, the F70 fell victim to Fokker's serious business problems. A total of only 47 F70s were built between 1994 and 1997.

The third product to arrive was Embraer's EMB-145 (now ERJ-145). From its confused design phase (three different configurations were tried), to its curious succession of order books, to its suspiciously just-in-time 're-launch order', this program provided one embarrassment after another. But ultimately, Embraer looks set to have the last laugh. Over 200 orders have been received, and in 1998 the –145 took almost 20% of the regional market, in terms of dollar value of deliveries.

Hopefully, these regional jets, and possibly some new ones, will permit additional cost improvements in the air transport system. And eventually, the world will regard air travel as another form of public transport.

Richard Aboulafia
Washington 1999

Aerospatiale/BAC Concorde (France, UK)

Passengers: 128

Development/History

Concorde is the only supersonic transport (SST) aircraft in the world. A four-engine narrow-body, it was designed and built by France's Aerospatiale and British Aircraft Corporation (now BAe). The first test aircraft flew in March 1969. The Concorde entered service in January 1976. Flying supersonic costs more than twice what first class subsonic passengers pay. The predicted market for the Concorde was 200 aircraft. The reality is that 16 were sold to Air France and British Airways. Both airlines still use most of these aircraft. The Concorde will remain in service until around 2010.

Variants

Concorde: Four-engined narrow-bodied supersonic transport

Status

Production completed

Operators

Air France, British Airways

Specifications (Concorde)

Powerplant

Four Rolls-Royce/SNECMA Olympus 593 Mk 602 turbojets, each rated at 169.3 kN (38,050 lbst)

Dimensions

Length: 61.66 m (202 ft 3.6 in)
Height: 1.96 m (6ft 5in)
Wing span: 25.56 m (83 ft 10in)

Weights

Empty operating: 78,700 kg (173,500 lb);
MTOW: 185,065 kg (408,000 lb)

Performance

Cruise speed: 2,179 km/h (1,176 kts)
Range: 6,380 km (3,970 nm)

At twenty-three years old, the world's only supersonic transport, the Concorde, still captures the imagination

Airbus A300 (France, Germany, Spain, UK)

Passengers: 250 (three class)

Development/History

A mid-sized medium-range jetliner, the A300 was the first wide-body twinjet. It was also the first plane built by the Airbus consortium. Airbus began in 1965 as an Anglo-French project, and later grew into the French/German/British/Spanish effort, with final production facilities in Toulouse, France. First proposed in 1968, the A300 made its first flight in October 1972. The A300 entered service, with Air France, in May 1974. The A300B2 and B4 were the first two variants. Airbus built 248 of these, with production ending in late 1984. They were replaced by the current A300-600, also available as the extended-range-600R. The —600 features a two-crew flight deck, increased passenger and freight capacity, and other improvements. Airbus is also building four huge A300-600ST Super Transporters to move aerostructures between production facilities.

Specifications (A300-600R)

Powerplant
Two GE CF6 or Pratt & Whitney PW4158 turbofans

Data below is for aircraft with CF6-80C2A5s, each rated at 273.6kN (61,500 lbst)

Dimensions
Length: 54.08 m (177 ft 5 in)
Height: 16.53 m (54 ft 3 in)
Wing span: 44.84 m (147 ft 1 in)

Weights
Empty operating: 89, 813 kg (198,003 lb);
MTOW: 170,500 kg (375,885 lb)

Performance
Cruise speed: 875 km/h (472 kts)
Range: 7,410 km (4,000 nm)

Variants

A300B2/B4: Large-capacity wide-bodied medium/long-range commercial airliner
A300-600: Updated version with new cockpit
A300-600R: Extended range version of A300-600 with higher maximum T-O weight
A300-600F: Cargo version
A300-600ST: Oversize freight transport

Status

In production
A300B2/B4 ended production in late 1984

Operators

Egyptair, China Airlines, China Eastern Airlines, Japan Air System, Korean Air, Pakistan International Airlines Philippine Airlines, Saudi Arabian Airlines, Thai International, Air France, Alitalia, Iberia, Lufthansa, American Airlines, FedEx

The A300 was the first aircraft built by Airbus and thus launched the Euro-American air wars

A310 (France, Germany, Spain, UK)

Passengers: 210 (three class)

Development/History

The A310 was first proposed in the early 1970s as the A300B10. The A310 program was launched in July 1978. The first prototype flew in April 1982. Simultaneous French and German certification was awarded in March 1983. The A310 is available with a choice of either GE or Pratt & Whitney engines. The A310 is built in two basic variants, the −200 and the −300 extended range version. The A310-200 is the basic passenger model and the −200F is the freighter.

Variants

A310-200: Large-capacity wide-bodied medium/extended-range transport
A310-300: Extended-range passenger version

Status

Minimal production forecast through 2000

Operators

Air Afrique, Air India, Emirates Airlines, Pakistan International Airlines, Singapore Airlines, Aeroflot Russian International Airlines, Air France, Lufthansa, Swissair, THY-Turkish Airlines, Air Jamaica, FedEx

Specifications (A310-300)

Powerplant

Two GE CF6 or Pratt & Whitney PW4152 turbofans

Data below is for aircraft with CF6-80C2A2s, each rated at 238 kN (53,500 lbst)

Dimensions

Length: 46.66 m (153 ft 1 in);
Height: 15.8 m (51 ft 10in)
Wing span: 43.89 m (144 ft)

Weights

Empty operating: 80,344 kg (177,128 lb);
MTOW: 150,000 kg (330,695 lb)

Performance

Cruise speed: 875 km/h (472 kts)
Range: 7,982 km (4,310 nm)

Uzbekistan winging its way into the West with an A310

A310 (France, Germany, Spain, UK)

The A310-300 is the extended range version

A320 (France, Germany, Spain, UK)

Passengers: 150 (two class)

Development/History

The A320 was Airbus's first narrow-body jetliner. Designed to carry 150 passengers on short-to-medium routes, the A320 competes with Boeing's 737 and MD-80/90. Airbus designed the A320 with fly-by-wire controls and 15% composite materials content. Airbus also gave customers a choice of engines — GE/SNECMA's CFM56 or International Aero Engines' V2500. The launch order came from Pan Am, which fortunately did not doom the program. The A320 made its first flight in 1987. Airbus has built over 600 A320s, with production continuing.

Specifications (A320-200)

Powerplant
Two CFM International CFM56-5 or International Aero Engines V2500-A1 turbofans

Data below is for aircraft with CFM56-5A1s, each rated at 1111.2 kN (25,000 lbst)

Dimensions
Length: 37.57 m (123 ft 3 in)
Height: 11.80m (38 ft 8.5 in)
Wing span: 33.91 m (111 ft 3 in)

Weights
Empty operating: 41,782 kg (92,113 lb);
MTOW: 75,500 kg (166,449 lb)

Performance
Cruise speed: 903 km/h (487 kts)
Range: 5,000 km (2,700 nm)

The A320 was Airbus' first narrow-body airliner

A320 (France, Germany, Spain, UK)

Variants

A320-100: Initial version, twin-turbofan short/medium-range airliner

A320-200: Twin-turbofan short/medium-range airliner with wingtip fences, wing centre-section fuel tank and higher maximum T-O weight

Status

In production

Operators

Eyptair, South African Airways, Tunis Air, All Nippon Airways, Ansett Australia, China Southern Airlines, Indian Airlines, Air France, British Midland Airways, Iberia, Lufthansa, Sissair, TAP-Air Portugal, Air Canada, America West Airlines, Northwest Airlines, United Airlines

From Ansett Australia to United Airlines, the A320 proves a popular choice worldwide

A319/321 (France,Germany,Spain,UK)

Passengers: 124 (two class)

Development/History

The A319 and 321 are, respectively, the shortened and stretched versions of Airbus's A320 narrow-body jetliner. Both use the same systems, wings and engine selection as the 150-seat A320. Airbus realized that will to fuselage plugs and some modifications, it could create a 186-seat competitor to the Boeing 757. The A321 made its first flight in March 1993, followed by European JAA certification in December. The 124-seat A319 is a more recent effort, first conceived in the early 1990s. Airbus launched the A319 with only six firm orders from ILFC in June 1993. The A319 entered service in May 1996.

Specifications (A319)

Powerplant
Two CFM International CFM56-5 or International Aero Engines V2522-A5 turbofans.

Data below is for aircraft with CFM56-5A4s, each rated at 97.9 kN (22,000 lbst)

Dimensions
Length: 33.80 m (110 ft 11 in)
Height: 11.80 m (38 ft 8.5 in)
Wing span: 33.91 m (111 ft 3 in)

Weights
Empty operating: 40,125 kg (88,460 lb);
MTOW: 64,000 kg (141,095 lb)

Performance
Cruise speed: 903 km/h (487 kts);
Range: 5,000 km (1,900 nm)

Variants

A319: Shortened version of A320 twin-turbofan short/medium-range airliner
A319CJ: Corporate jetliner version
A321-100: Stretched version of A320 twin-turbofan short/medium-range airliner
A321-200: Extended range version with higher thrust versions of existing engines and additional centre tank (106-seat model, under consideration)

Status

In production

Operators

Air France, Croatia Airlines, Lufthansa, Swissair, TAP-Air Portugal, Air Canada, United Airlines

The A321 is the stretched version of the A320

Lower number, shortened version of the A320, the A319 also comes as a corporate jetliner

A330 (France, Germany, Spain, UK)

Passengers: 335 (three class)

Development/History

The A330 is a twin-engine medium-range wide-body jetliner built by the Airbus consortium. Closely related to the four-engine A340, the A330 holds 335 passengers in a three class configuration. Airbus launched the A330/340 program in June 1987. The A330 was rolled out in Toulouse in October 1992, followed by a first flight in November. On October 21, 1993 the A330 became the first airliner to obtain joint US/European FAA/JAA certification. In late 1993 Airbus delivered the first production A330 to France's Air Inter. The first production model is the A330-300, which competes with the Boeing 767/777 and MD-11. Airbus is considering stretched and shortened versions of the A330.

Variants

A330-300: Wide-body medium/long-range twin-engined airliner
A330-200: Extended-range, shortened version

Status

In production

Specifications (A330-300)

Powerplant
Two GE CF6-80E1A2, Pratt & Whitney PW4164/4168, or Rolls-Royce Trent 768/772 turbofans.

Data below is for aircraft with DF6-80E1A2s each rated at 300.3 kN (67,500 lbst).

Dimensions
Length: 63.65 m (208 ft 10 in)
Height: 12.92 m (42 ft 5 in)
Wing span: 45.23 m (148 ft 5 in)

Weights
Empty operating: 120,285 kg (265,183 lb);
MTOW: 212,000 kg (467,379 lb)

Performance
Cruise speed: 850 km/h (459 kts)
Range: 8,334 km (4,500 nm)

The A330 is the first jetliner to receive joint FAA/JAA certification

A330 (France, Germany, Spain, UK)

Operators
Cathay Pacific Airways, Emirates Airlines, Garuda Indonesia, Malaysia Airlines, Thai International, Air France, LTU, Swissair, Northwest Airlines, Trans World Airlines

The medium-range wide-body A330 jetliner competes with the Boeing 767/777

A340 (France, Germany, Spain, UK)

Passengers: 295 (three class)

Development/History

The A340, Airbus's first four-engine design, is a long-range wide-body competing with Boeing's 777 and MD-11 in the mini-jumbo market. It is closely related to the A330, the main difference being the propulsion philosophy (two big engines versus four medium ones). Many A330/340 systems and most of the fuselage and wings are identical. Originally known as the A300B11/TA11, the A340 program was launched in June 1987. Its first flight was in October 1991. The A340 received European JAA certification in December 1992 and entered service in March 1994. Airbus launched two stretches of the A340, the 310-seat A340-500 at the 1997 Paris Air Show, and the major stretch, the 380-seat A340-600 was launched with an order in December 1997.

Specifications (A340-300)

Powerplant
Four CFM International (GE/SNECMA) CFM56-2-C1 turbofans, each rated at 97.9 kN (22,000 lbst)

Dimensions
Length: 57.12 m (187 ft 5 in)
Height: 12.92 m (42 ft 5 in)
Wing span: 45.23 m (148 ft 5 in)

Weights
Empty operating: 75,500 kg (166,500 lb);
MTOW: 161,025 kg (355,000 lb)

Performance
Cruise speed: 850 km/h (459 kts)
Range: 8,950 km (4,830 nm)

Variants

A340: Large-capacity wide-bodied medium/long-range airliner

A340-200: Short-fuselage, longer-range version of A340-300

A340-300: Four-engined higher-capacity version

A340-500: Ultra-long-range variant, able to carry 313 passengers in three classes

A340-600: Derivative of A340-300 with fuselage stretch, additional fuel capacity, Trent 500 engines, and 365,000 kg maximum T-O weight

Status

In production

Operators

Air Mauritius, All Nippon Airways, Cathay Pacific Airways, China Eastern Airlines, Singapore Airlines, Air France, Iberia, Lufthansa, Virgin Atlantic Airways, Air Canada

The A340 was Airbus' first four-engine design

The A340-600 is a stretched version seating 380 passengers

ATR 42/72 (France, Italy)

Passengers: 42

Development/History

The ATR series comprises two twin turboprop Regional Transport Aircraft (ATR in French and Italian) developed and built by France's Aerospatiale and Italy's Alenia. The ATR 42 seats 42-50, while the stretched ATR 72 seats 70-80. The aircraft are high-wing pressurized designs, with digital avionics. ATRs can be distinguished from similar aircraft (Fokker 50, DHC Dash 8) by their landing gear, which retracts inside the

Specifications (ATR 42-300)

Powerplant
Two Pratt & Whitney Canada PW120 turboprops, each rated at 1,342 kW (1,800 shp)

Dimensions
Length: 22.67 m (74 ft 5.4 in)
Height: 7.586 m (24 ft 10.75 in)
Wing span: 24.57 m (80 ft 7.5 in)

Weights
Empty operating: 10,285 kg (22,674 lb)
MTOW: 16,700 kg (36,817 lb)

Performance
Cruise speed: 498 km/h (269 kts)
Range: 1,944 km (1,050 nm)

The ATR, Franco-Italian cooperation at its finest

fuselage, not the engine nacelles. The ATR 42 was launched in October 1981 and entered service in December 1985. The ATR 72 program began in January 1986. The type flew in October 1988, entering service one year later. It is also available with uprated engines for hot-and-high operations as the ATR 72-210. ATR production is continuing, and as of late 1998 ATR had delivered over 330 ATR 42s and 190 ATR 72s.

Variants
ATR 42-300: Pressurized twin-turboprop regional transport
ATR 72-200: Stretched version
Proposed ATR 52C: Military cargo version

Status
In production

Operators
Simmons, Continental Express, Eurowings, Transasia, Mount Cook AL, Brit Air, Avianova, City Flyer Express

The ATR 42 and 72 in flight demonstrate how their landing gear retract inside the fuselage rather than the engine nacelles

Boeing 707 (US)

Passengers: 147 (two class)

Development/History

The 707 was the first truly successful effort to design an efficient, large capacity jetliner capable of crossing the Atlantic. The 707 introduced the thin, swept wing with podded engines underneath that we take for granted today. A four-engine long-range narrow-body design, the 707 began as Boeing's Model 367-80, a prototype that flew in July 1954. The first model, the 707-120, was certified in September 1958. It entered service with Pan Am one month later. First 707 versions used Pratt & Whitney JT3C turbojets, followed by JT4As. In 1960 Boeing introduced JT3D turbofans as an option. These later became standard, but Boeing also built the 707-420, powered by Rolls-Royce Conways. The last commercial version was delivered to Morocco in 1982. The 707 also found extensive use for military applications, most notably as an AWACS radar plane. The production line for these versions closed in April 1991. Final count: 1,010 707s.

Specifications (707-320C)

Powerplant
Four Pratt & Whitney JT3D-7 turbofans, each rated at 84.5 kN (19,000 lbst)

Dimensions
Length: 46.61 m (152 ft 11 in)
Height: 12.93 m (42 ft 5 in)
Wing span: 44.92 m (145 ft 9 in)

Weights
Empty operating: 66,406 kg (146,400 lb);
MTOW: 151,315 kg (333,600 lb)

Performance
Cruise speed: 973 km/h (525 kts)
Range: 9,265 km (5,000 nm)

Variants

707-120: Four-engine long-range narrow-body airliner

707-320: Intercontinental version with longer fuselage, bigger wing and higher-powered engines

707-420: Powered by Rolls-Royce Conway engines

Status

Production completed

Operators

Air Atlantic Cargo, Angola Air Charter, Zaire Express, Iran Air, Kuwait Airways, Middle East Airlines, TMA, Azerbaijan Airlines, JARO International, AECA, Beta Cargo, Millon Air

A Boeing 707, the "Original", testing its trans-Atlantic wings

Boeing 707 (US)

Over land as well as sea, the 707 marked the beginning of an era

Boeing 717 (f/k/a MD-95) (US)

Passengers: 100 (two class)

Development/History

The Boeing 717, formerly known as the McDonnell Douglas MD-95 before the merger, is a narrow-body twinjet designed for short/medium-range routes. Essentially a reincarnation of the DC-9-30, the Boeing 717 has new avionics and Rolls-Royce/BMW BR715 turbofans. It seats 106 passengers in two classes, or 129 in one class. First announced as the MD-95 in 1991, as a joint venture with China's CATIC. The Chinese-US manufacturing plan fell through, but Douglas continued to market the aircraft. After many false starts, the MD-95 was launched in October 1995 with a 50 firm and 50 option order from the now defunct Valujet discount carrier.

Variants

717-200: 100-passenger twin-turbofan transport

Status

Beginning production

Operators

AirTran (50 on order)

Specifications (Boeing 717-200)

Powerplant
Two BMW/Rolls-Royce BR715 turbofans, each rated at 82.29 kN (18,500 lbst)

Dimensions
Length: 36.36 m (119 ft 3.5 in)
Height: 8.60 m (28 ft 2.5 in)
Wing span: 28.44 m (93 ft 3.5 in)

Weights
Empty operating: 30,073 kg (66,300 lb)
MTOW: 51,710 kg (114,000 lb)

Performance
Cruise speed: 811 km/h (438 kts)
Range: 2,778 km (1,500 nm)

Boeing 717 (f/k/a MD-95) (US)

A jetliner by any other name, still has the same customers

Boeing 727 (US)

Passengers: 145 (two class), 189 (all economy)

Development/History

The 727, a 145-seat three-engine transport for
domestic trunk routes, was Boeing's second
jetliner after the 707. After examining the
alternatives, Boeing decided to use a rear-
engine trijet configuration, an idea borrowed
from the smaller Hawker Siddeley Trident. All
727s are powered by members of the Pratt &
Whitney JT8D family and have a three-crew
flight deck. The 727 program was launched in
December 1960. A prototype flew in February
1963. The first 727 was the -100, a 131-seat
model powered by JT8D-1s. The -100 was also
available as the -100C, a convertible
cargo/passenger model, and the -100QC, a
Quick Change cargo version. The 145-seat
stretched -200 was certified in November 1967.
It became the standard 727. The last variant
was the pure-freight 727F, delivered in 1983.
Boeing built a total of 1,832 727s, including
one test aircraft. Of these, 1,245 were 727-200s
and 15 were 727Fs. The last 727 was delivered
in September 1984.

Specifications (727-200)

Powerplant
Three Pratt & Whitney JT8D-9A turbofans, each flat rated at 64.5 kN
(14,5000 lbst); also available with the uprated JT8D-11, -15, -17 and −17R.

Dimensions
Length: 46.69 m (153 ft 2 in)
Height: 10.36 m (34 ft)
Wing span: 32.92 m (108 ft)

Weights
Empty operating: 45,360 kg (100,000 lb)
MTOW: 83,820 kg (184,800 lb)

Performance
Cruise speed: 872 km/h (471 kts)
Range: 3,706 km (2,000 nm)

Boeing 727 (US)

Variants

727-100: 131-seat three-engine transport
727-100C: Convertible cargo/passenger version
727-100QC: Quick Change cargo version
727-200: 145-seat stretched version
727F: Freighter version

Status

Production completed

Boeing's second at bat delivered 822 more aircraft than its first

Operators

Blue Airlines, Kabo Airlines, TransAfrik, Triax Airlines, Mahfooz Aviation, European Air Transport, Olympic Airways, Star Air, DHL Airways, FedEx, Kelowna Flightcraft, Morningstar Air Express, Ryan International Airlines, Trans World Airlines, United Parcel Service, US Airways Shuttle, Air Algerie, Libyan Arab Airlines, Tunis Air, Iran Air, Iraqi Airways, Syrianair, Yemenia, European Air Transport, Iberia, JAT, American Airlines, American Trans Air, Aviacsa, Continental Airlines, Delta Air Lines, Mexicana, Northwest Airlines, United Parcel Service

The 727 was exclusively powered by the Pratt & Whitney JT8D family

Boeing 737-100/200 (US)

Passengers: \120-130 (two class)

Development/History

The legendary 737 series began with the 737-100 version, a 'Baby Boeing' carrying 100 passengers on short routes. Boeing began the 737-100 program in November 1964, even though the similar BAC 1-11 and Douglas DC-9 programs were well underway. The early 737s were powered by Pratt & Whitney JT8D engines. In February 1965 Lufthansa placed a launch order for 21 737-100s. A prototype flew in April 1967. Meanwhile, Boeing decided to stretch the 737, creating the 120/130-seat 737-200. United launched this version in April 1965, and a 737-200 flew in August 1967. The 737-100 and -200 were certified in December 1967. The -100 entered service in February 1968, followed by the -200 in April 1968. By 1981, annual production rose to 108 aircraft. Boeing delivered the last 737-200 in 1988.

Specifications (737-200)

Powerplant
Three Pratt & Whitney JT8D-9A turbofans, each rated at 64.5 kN (14,500 lbst)

Dimensions
Length: 46.60 m (153 ft 2 in)
Height: 10.36 m (34 ft 0 in)
Wing span: 32.92 m (108 ft 0 in)

Weights
Empty operating: 45.360 kg (100,000 lb)
MTOW: 83,820 kg (184,800 lb)

Performance
Cruise speed: 856 km/h (462 kts)
Range: 3,437 km (1,855 nm)

Variants

737-100: Twin-turbofan airliner

737-200: Twin-turbofan airliner with max T-O weight of 52,390 kg and accommodation for 120 passengers and baggage

737-200C: Convertible cargo version with strengthened fuselage and floor, and large two-position upper deck cargo door

Status

Production completed

A 737-200 is the "Baby Boeing" stretched

Boeing 737-100/200 (US)

Operators

Air Algerie, Nigeria Airways, South African Airways, Air New Zealand, Air Nippon, Bouraq Indonesia, Indian Airlines, Japan TransOcean Air, Mandala Airlines, Saudi Arabian Airlines, Air France, British Airways, Olympic Airways, Ryanair, Aerolineas Argentianas, Aloha, America West Airlines, Canadian Airlines International, Continental Airlines, Delta Air Express, LAN Chile, Southwest Airlines, United Airlines, US Airways, Vasp

The last 737-200 was delivered in 1988

Boeing 737-300/400/500 (US)

Passengers: 128 (two class)

Development/History

Boeing's second generation of 737s was launched in March 1981. The second series features all-new engines, wing modifications, and a new flight deck. It competes with Airbus's A320 and McDonnell Douglas's MD-80 series. The first new 737 was the -300, launched in March 1981. Stretched to seat 128 passengers in two classes, the -300 flew in February 1984 and was certified in November 1984. Two years later, Boeing launched the 737-400, a 146-seat stretch. It entered service in September 1988. Finally, Boeing launched the shortened 108-seat 737-500 in May 1987. It entered service in March 1990. The second 737 series has proven even more popular than the 737-100/200. As of late 1995 Boeing had delivered over 1,600 737-300/400/500s. Production of all three current 737s is continuing, but slowing.

Specifications (737-300)

Powerplant
Two CFM International CFM56-3C-1 turbofans rated at 88.97 kN (20,000 lbst)

Dimensions
Length: 33.40 m (109 ft 7 in)
Height: 11.13 m (36 ft 6 in)
Wing span: 28.88 m (94 ft 9 in)

Weights
Empty operating: 31,895 kg (70,320 lb)
MTOW: 56,472 kg (124,500 lb)

Performance
Cruise speed: 794 km/h (429 kts)
Range: 4,554 km (2,830 nm)

Boeing 737-300/400/500 (US)

Boeing's second-generation of 737s takes off

Variants

737-300: Twin-turbofan airliner
737-400: Stretched version of 737-300, seats from 146-168 passengers
737-500: Short-body version of 737-300, seats from 108-138 passengers

Status

In production through 2001

Operators

Kenya Aiways, Air China, Ansett Australia, China Southwest Airlines, China Yunnan Airlines, Garuda Indonesia, Philippine Airlines, Qantas, SilkAir, Air Europe, Deutsche BA, KLM Royal Dutch Airlines, Lufthansa, TAP-Air Portugal, Virgin Express, America West Airlines, Continental Airlines, Southwest Airlines, United Airlines, US Airways, Varig, Western Pacific Airlines, Royal Air Moroc, Asiana Airlines, Japan Airlines, Jet Airways, Malaysia Airlines, Qantas, Thai International, Aeroflot Russian International Airlines, British Airways, Hapag-Lloyd, KLM Royal Dutch Airlines, THY-Turkish Airlines, Alaska Airlines, US Airways, Tunis Air, Air Nippon, Aer Lingus, CSA, Maersk Air, Rio Sul

The 737-300/400/500 proved to be more popular than either the 737-100 or -200

Boeing 737-600/700/800 (US)

Passengers: 128 (two class)

Development/History

Boeing is now working on a third 737 generation designed to replace the 737-300/400/500. Specifically, the 108-seat 737-600 will replace the -500, the 146-seat -700 will replace the -300, and the 160-seat -800 will replace the -400. Boeing announced the 737-X series in June 1993. In November 1993 Southwest Airlines launched the 737-700 with 63 firm and 63 option orders. The next to be launched was the -800. The new 737 series will feature quieter and more efficient CFM56-7 versions of the CFM56-3 engines used on the current 737s. They should permit the new 737s to have operating costs 15% lower than the current series, and to meet Stage 4 noise regulations. The next 737s will also have bigger wings, new avionics, and more flexible interiors. Thanks to these efforts, the 737 family will probably still be in production in 2015, its 50th continuous year.

Specifications (737-700)

Powerplant
Two CFM International CFM56-7 turbofans each rated at 106.76 kN (24,000 lbst)

Dimensions
Length: 33.63 m (110 ft 4 in)
Height: 11.13 m (36 ft 6 in)
Wing span: 34.31 m (112 ft 7 in)

Weights
Empty operating: 31,895 kg (70,320 lb)
MTOW: 67,585 kg (149,000 lb)

Performance
Cruise speed: Mach 0.80
Range: 5,556 km (3,000 nm)

Opposite: Three's a charm for Boeing's 737 series

Boeing 737-600/700/800 (US)

Variants

737-600: Twin-turbofan airliner, seating 110 two-class passengers
737-700: Twin-turbofan airliner, seating 126 two-class passengers
737-700IGW: Increased gross weight version
737-800: Stretched version, seating 162 two-class passengers

Status

In production

Operators

SAS, Continental Airlines, Braathens SAFE, Germania, Continental Airlines, Southwest Airlines, Royal Air Maroc, China Airlines, Air Europa, Hapag-Lloyd, Transavia Airlines, American Airlines, Delta Air Lines

The new 737 series features quieter and more efficient CFM56-7 engines

The 737-700 getting an escort

Boeing 747-100/200/300 (US)

Passengers: 452 (three class)

Development/History

'Building A Legend' says the banner above Boeing's 747 assembly line. The banner is right. The 747 is the largest commercial jetliner in the world. It was also the first wide-body airliner, making it possible for vast numbers of people to travel cheaply to distant parts of the world. The 747 story began in the 1960s, when Boeing lost a US Air Force competition to build a large transport. The company offered its design as a civil jetliner. Pan Am launched the program in April 1966. The 747 was certified in December 1969. The first model was the 747-100, powered by Pratt & Whitney JT9D turbofans. It was followed by the longer range -200, which entered service in 1971. The -300 featured a stretched upper deck. It entered service in 1983.

Variants

747-100: Wide-body airliner, with 710,000 lb MTOW

747-200: Variant with higher weights, new engines

747-300: Variant with extended upper deck

Specifications (747-200B)

Powerplant

Four GE CF6-80C2, Pratt & Whitney PW4000 or Rolls-Royce RB.211-524 turbofans.

Data below is for aircraft with PW4056s rated at 258 kN (57,900 lbst).

Dimensions

Length: 68.6 m (225 ft 2 in)
Height: 19.3 m (63 ft 4 in)
Wing span: 57 m (195.7 ft)

Weights

Empty operating: 172,620 kg (383,600 lb)
MTOW: 374,850 kg (833,000 lb)

Performance

Cruise speed: 522-527 kts
Range: 6,350-6,900 nm

Status

Production completed

Operators

South African Airways, Air China, All Nippon Airways, Saudi Arabian Airlines, British Airways, Polar Air Cargo, United Airlines, United Parcel Service, Air India, Cathay Pacific Airways, Japan Airlines, Korean Air, Nippon Cargo Airlines, Air France, KLM Royal Dutch Airlines, Lufthansa Cargo Airlines, Atlas Air, Northwest Airlines, Egyptair, South African Airways, Swissair, Varig

The legend begins

Rolling out the 747 with all the bells and whistles

Boeing 747-400 (US)

Passengers: 421 (three class)

Development/History

The current version of the 747 is the 747-400, which is distinguished by winglets. It also has greater range and wider wings than its predecessors, as well as an advanced two-crew flight deck. It is available in cargo and combi variants. Boeing is considering several new stretched and re-winged variants for the future. The 747 remains the bellwether of the industry.

Variants

747-400: Wide-body airliner, basic passenger version with standard and three optional gross weights, -400 series distinguished by winglets

747-400M Combi: Passenger/freight version; maximum 266 three-class passengers with freight, 413 without freight

747-400F: All-freight version

747-400X/IGW: Proposed heavier version with one or two additional fuel tanks in hold; structural strengthening around centrebody, wing/fuselage joint, flaps and landing gear

Specifications (747-400)

Powerplant

Four GE CF6-80C2, Pratt & Whitney PW4000 or Rolls-Royce RB.211-524 turbofans.

Data below is for aircraft with PW4056s rated at 258 kN (57,900 lbst).

Dimensions

Length: 70.66 m (231 ft 10 in)
Height: 1941 m (63 ft 8 in)
Wing span: 64.92 m (213 ft)

Weights

Empty operating: 180,985 kg (399,000 lb)
MTOW: 391,500 kg (870,000 lb)

Performance

Cruise speed: 940 km/h (507 kts)
Range: 13,278 km (7,165 nm)

Boeing 747-400 (US)

Status
In production
747-400X/IGW-on offer

Operators
South African Airways, Air China, All Nippon Airways, Cathay Pacific Airways, Japan Airlines, Korean Air, Malaysia Airlines, Qantas, Singapore Airlines, Thai International, British Airways, Lufthansa, Atlas Air, Untied Airlines

The 747-400, the current version, has a greater range and an advanced two-crew flight deck

The 747-400 is distinguished by winglets

Boeing 757 (US)

Passengers: 186 (two class)

Development/History

The 757 is a medium-range twinjet airliner designed for transcontinental operations. The largest narrow-body built, the 757 can carry up to 220 passengers. Boeing created the 757 as a successor to the 727. It launched the program in August 1978. The 757 was rolled out in January 1982, and made its first flight one month later. It entered service in January 1983. The first version was the 757-200. It remains the current production model, and is available as a cargo aircraft. A stretched 757-300 arrived in May 1998. The 757 fuselage is basically the same used on Boeing's 707, 727, and 737. The 757 can be powered by a choice of Rolls-Royce or Pratt & Whitney engines, and was one of the first planes to use a two-crew flight deck.

Variants

757-200: Medium-range twin-turbofan airliner
757-200PF: Package freighter version with large freight door forward, single crew doors and no windows
757-200M Combi: Mixed cargo/passenger

Specifications (757-200)

Powerplant
Two Rolls-Royce RB.211-535E4 turbofans each rated at 178.4 kN (40,100 lbst)

Dimensions
Length: 47.32 (155 ft 3 in)
Height: 13.56 m (44 ft 6 in)
Wing span: 38.05 m (124 ft 10 in)

Weights
Empty operating: 57,180 kg (126,060 lb)
MTOW: 99,790 kg (220,000 lb)

Performance
Cruise speed: 851 km/h (459 kts)
Range: 5,222 km (2,820 nm)

version with windows, upward-opening cargo door to port (forward)
757-200F: Freighter version
757-300: Stretched version of 757-200

Status
In production

Operators
Ethiopian Airlines, China Southern Airlines, China Southwest Airlines, El Al, Shanghai Airlines, Air 2000, Air Holland, Airtours International, Britannia Airways, British Airways, Condor Flugdienst, Iberia, LTU, Monarch Airlines, America West Airlines, American Airlines, American Trans Air, Continental Airlines, Delta Air Lines, Northwest Airlines, Trans World Airlines, United Airlines, United Parcel Service, US Airways

The USAF operates the 757-200 as the C-32A

The 757 was one of the first planes to use a two-crew flight deck

Boeing 767 (US)

Passengers: 260 (210 on −300ER)

Development/History

The 767 is Boeing's smallest wide-body, a 220-270 passenger twinjet which competes with (and resembles) Airbus's A310. The 767 first flew in September 1981. First deliveries came in August 1982. The first 767 was the -200, but a stretched 767-300 was launched in September 1983. The -300 is 21 ft (6.4 m) longer, but is otherwise similar to the -200. Most production today is for the 767-300. Both models are available as extended range variants, as the -200ER/-300ER. ER variants include larger wing centre-section fuel tanks, and structural changes needed to support the extra weight. The 767 is available with a choice of General Electric, Pratt & Whitney, or Rolls-Royce turbofans. Most of the fuselage is built in Japan by Kawasaki and Mitsubishi. The 767 was the first Boeing plane to use a two-crew flight deck with electronic flight instrument systems (EFIS). Seating is usually seven or eight abreast.

Specifications (767-300)

Powerplant
Two GE CF6-80C2, Pratt Whitney PW4050/4052, or Rolls-Royce RB.211-524G turbofans.

Data below is for 767-300s with CF6-80C2B2s, each rated at 233.5 kN (52,500 lbst).

Dimensions
Length: 54.9 m (180 ft 3 in)
Height: 15.9 m (52 ft)
Wing span: 47.6 m (156 ft 1 in)

Weights
Empty operating: 86,953 kg (191,700 lb)
MTOW: 156,490 kg (345,000 lb)

Performance
Cruise speed: 850 km/h (459 kts)
Range: 7,450 km (4,020 nm)

Boeing 767 (US)

Boeing's smallest wide-body, the 767, touches down

Variants

767-200: Medium/long-range twin-turbofan airliner
767-300: Stretched 269-passenger version of 767-200
7676-200ER: Extended Range version of 767-200
767-300ER: Extended Range, higher gross weight version of 767-300
767-300F: Freighter version

Status

In production

Operators

Air Algerie, Air China, All Nippon Airways, Ansett Australia, Qantas, Britannia Airways, Air Canada, American Airlines, Delta Air Lines, Trans World Airlines, United Airlines, US Airways, Japan Airlines, British Airways

The 767-300 is the stretched version of the 767

Boeing 777 (US)

Passengers: 305-328 (three class)

Development/History

The last new large jetliner entering service this century, the Triple Seven is a wide-body twinjet seating 300-350 passengers, the 777 is designed for intercontinental and transcontinental routes. It fills the gap in Boeing's product line between the 767 and 747. Boeing announced the 767-X project in June 1989. The new plane was redesignated 777 after its launch in October 1990. The first 777 flew in June 1994. It was certified in April 1995. The 777 is available with a choice of General Electric, Pratt & Whitney, or Rolls-Royce turbofans. It is the first application for GE's GE90 engine. (Fun fact: the 777's engines, the most powerful aero engines ever built, are housed in nacelles as wide as a 737's fuselage). Japanese industry also has a considerable stake in the 777 project, building most of the 777's fuselage. The 777-300 stretch variant entered service in 1998 and seats up to 440 passengers and will require engines rated up to 436 kN (98,000 lbst).

Specifications (777-200A)

Powerplant
Two GE GE90, Pratt & Whitney PW4000 or Rolls-Royce Trent 800 turbofans.

Data below is for aircraft with PW4074s rated at 329.17 kN (74,000 lbst).

Dimensions
Length: 63.73 m (209 ft 1 in)
Height: 18.51 m (60 ft 9 in)
Wing span: 60.93 m (199 ft 11 in)

Weights
Empty operating: 135,580 kg (298,900 lb)
MTOW: 229,520 kg (506,000 lb)

Performance
Cruise speed: 897 km/h (484 kts)
Range: 7,505 km (4,050 nm)

The 777 can transport up to 350 people over 7,500 km

Boeing 777 (US)

Variants

777-200: Long-range high-capacity twin-turbofan airliner with maximum T-O weight of 229,520 kg, seating 305-440 passengers depending on configuration
777-200A: Long-range high-capacity twin-turbofan airliner
777-200X: Ultra-long-range version, seating

298 passengers
777-200IGW: Increased gross weight version
777-300: Stretched version, featuring strengthened airframe, inboard wing and landing gear, ground manoeuvring cameras on horizontal tail surfaces and wing/fuselage fairing

Because of its range, the Triple Seven is popular among South Pacific airlines

Status
In production

Operators
All Nippon Airways, Singapore Airlines, Saudi Arabian Airlines, Air France, British Airways, American Airlines, Continental Airlines, United Airlines, Asiana Airlines, Cathay Pacific Airways, Korean Air, Thai International

At home as much in urban as island landscapes

Boeing MD-11 (US)

Passengers: 293 (three class)

Development/History

The Boeing MD-11 is a three-engined long-range wide-body jetliner derived from the DC-10. Design work began on a mere stretch of the older design, known as the DC-10 Series 50/60. As the project grew more ambitious, it was designated the MD-100, and in 1984, the MD-11. FAA certification was awarded in November 1990. Compared with the DC-10, the MD-11 has a 5.66 m (18 ft 7 in) fuselage stretch, larger wings, more power engines, and a two-crew cockpit. As with the DC-10, the MD-11 is offered with a choice of General Electric or Pratt & Whitney engines. The MD-11 is available in freighter, convertible freighter, and combi variants.

Specifications (MD-11)

Powerplant
Three Pratt & Whitney PW4460 or GE CF6-80C2 turbofans.

Data below is for aircraft with PW4460s, each rated at 266.9 kN (60,000 lbst)

Dimensions
Length: 61.24 m (200 ft 11 in)
Height: 17.60 m (57 ft 9 in)
Wing span: 51.77 m (169 ft 10 in)

Weights
Empty operating: 131,035 kg (288,880 lb)
MTOW: 283,725 kg (625,500 lb)

Performance
Cruise speed: 898 km/h (560 kts)
Range: 12,607 km (6,803 nm)

Variants

MD-11: Medium/long-range airliner, seating 298 passengers in three-class layout

MD-11 Combi: Mixed cargo/passenger version for four to 10 cargo pallets and 168–240 passengers

MD-11CF: Convertible freighter version with main deck cargo door at front on port side

MD-11F: Freighter version; no cabin windows except observation windows

MD-11ER: Extended Range version offering either 480 nm greater range or 2,721 kg more payload

Emerging from the hangar

Boeing MD-11 (US)

Status
In production

Operators
China Eastern Airlines, Japan Airlines, Swissair,
American Airlines, Delta Air Lines, FedEx,
Varig, Vasp, KLM Royal Dutch Airlines

A MD-11 flies before the
Boeing takeover

64

Boeing MD-80 (USA)

Passengers: 155 (two class)

Development/History

The MD-80, a DC-9 derivative, was originally known as the DC-9 Super 80. Major changes from the DC-9 include new refanned Pratt & Whitney JT8D-200 series engines, a longer fuselage, and an increased wing span (28% greater than the DC-9-50). Renamed to reflect Douglas's status as part of McDonnell Douglas, the first MD-80 flew in October 1979. FAA certification was granted in August 1980, and the first production aircraft went to Swissair in September. There are five members of the MD-80 family: The MD-81, -82, -83, and -88 all seat 155 passengers. In June 1992, Douglas delivered its 1,024th MD-80, for a total of 2,000 twinjets including the DC-9. China's Shanghai Aviation Industrial Corp. (SAIC) built 35 MD-82s and -83s under license. The last of these was completed in August 1994. As this is written, production of the MD-80 is winding down. It is being replaced by the MD-90.

Specifications (MD-82)

Powerplant
Two Pratt & Whitney JT8D-217 turbofans, each rated at 89 kN (20,000 lbst)

Dimensions
Length: 45.06 m (147 ft 10 in)
Height: 9.19 m (30 ft 2 in)
Wing span: 32.87 m (107 ft 10 in)

Weights
Empty operating: 35,369 hg (77,976 lb)
MTOW: 67,812 kg (149,500 lb)

Performance
Cruise speed: 813 km/h (439 kts)
Range: 4,032 km (2,176 nm)

Boeing MD-80 (USA)

Variants

MD-81: Twin-turbofan short/medium-range airliner seating 172 passengers

MD-82: Powered by P&W JT8D-217s for hot and high performance and increased payload/range

MD-83: Extended range version

MD-87: Short-fuselage version for maximum 139 single-class passengers

MD-88: Combines JT8D-219 power plant with EFIS cockpit displays, flight management system, onboard windshear detection system and increased use of composites in structure

Status

In production

The MD-80 was originally known as the DC-9 Super 80

Operators

Nouvelair Tunisie, China
Eastern Airlines, China
Northern Airlines, Japan Air
System, Korean Air, Aero
Lloyd, Alitalia, AOM French
Airlines, Aviaco, Finnair,
Iberia, SAS, Spanair,
Aeromexico, Alaska Airlines,
American Airlines,
Continental Airlines, Delta
Air Lines, Reno Air, Trans
World Airlines, US Airways

An MD-UHB Demo lands

Boeing MD-90 (USA)

Passengers: 153 (two class)

Development/History

The MD-90, the third major incarnation of Douglas's twinjet family, was originally an innovative, high-tech design. However, economic conditions dictated that Douglas return to a traditional design. Douglas only committed to the MD-90-30, which seats 150-158 in a two-class configuration and would compete with the Boeing 737-300/-700 and the Airbus A320. Douglas had proposed several variants, including the shrunken MD-90-10 and the stretched MD-90-50. Following the merger with McDonnell Douglas, Boeing announced in November 1997 that it was killing both the MD-80 and MD-90 programs. Production is expected to end in 1999.

Variants

MD-90-30: Stretched MD-80 follow-on with lengthened fuselage (1.45 m) ahead of wing

Status

In production

Specifications (MD-90-30)

Powerplant
Two International Aero Engines V2525-D5 turbofans, each rated at 111.21 kN (25,000 lbst)

Dimensions
Length: 46.51 m (152 ft 7 in)
Height: 9.33 m (30 ft 7 in)
Wing span: 32.87 m (107 ft 10 in)

Weights
Empty operating: 40,007 kg (88,200 lb)
MTOW: 70,760 kg (156,000 lb)

Performance
Cruise speed: 809 km/h (437 kts)
Range: 4,200 km (2,266 nm)

Operators
CAAC, China Eastern
Airlines, Japan Air System,
Saudi Arabian Airlines, UNI
Air, Shenzhen Airlines, SAS,
Delta Air Lines, Reno Air

*Following the Boeing
merger, the MD-90's
future clouded and
production is to end along
with its predecessor*

The MD-90 flying in earlier clearer skies

Finally, the MD-90 grounded

British Aerospace 146/Avro RJ (UK)

Passengers: 100

Development/History

The 146/RJ is a four-engine 70-115 seat jetliner designed for short-haul operations. It is instantly identifiable as the only civil jetliner with a high wing (mounted above the fuselage). The 146/RJ has a complex history and nomenclature. It was designed as the Hawker Siddeley HS 146, but this project collapsed. When Hawker became part of BAe, it became the BAe 146. BAe relaunched the 146 in July 1978. It flew in September 1981 and entered service in May 1983. In June 1992 BAe renamed the series RJ (regional jet) followed by the seating capacity. The RJ70 and RJ85 uses the 146-100 airframe, while the RJ100 uses the 146-200 and the RJ115 uses the 146-300. RJs are also called Avroliners. The new RJs feature improved engines, new interiors, and digital avionics. The first RJ flew in March 1992, and deliveries began in late 1993. BAe built about 220 146s, and RJ production is continuing.

Specifications (Avro RJ100)

Powerplant
Four AlliedSignal LF507 turbofans, each rated at 31.14 kN (7,000 lbst)

Dimensions
Length: 28.6 m (93 ft 10 in)
Height: 8.61 m (28 ft 3 in)
Wing span: 26.21 m (86 ft 0 in)

Weights
Empty operating: 24,993 kg (55,100 lb)
MTOW: 46,039 kg (101,500 lb)

Performance
Cruise speed: 711 km/h (384 kts)
Range: 2,593 km/h (1,400 nm)

Variants

RJ100 (146-200 airframe): Four-turbofan short-range transport seating 110-116 passengers
RJ70 (146-100 airframe): Short fuselage version seating 70-94 passengers
RJ85 (146-100 airframe): Lengthened version for 85-112 passengers

Status

In production

Operators

TNT Express, Air Wisconsin, Air UK, Lufthansa, Cityline, Sabena, Crossair

With a history worthy of a Shakespearean play the Avro RJ finally took flight in 1992

Known first as the BAe 146 and later transformed into the Avro RJ, production of this short-haul jetliner continues

British Aerospace 748 & ATP/Jetstream 61 (UK)

Passengers: 60-72

Development/History

The 748 was designed by Britain's Avro company, later absorbed by British Aerospace. A low-wing twin turboprop pressurized design, the 748 was designed in the late 1950s. The first of two prototypes flew in June 1960 and the type entered service in 1962. The Series 1 was quickly followed by the Series 2, which flew in November 1961. The Series 2B had a larger wing and other improvements. The Series 2C, first flown in December 1971, featured a large freight door on the side of the fuselage. Final version was the Super 748, a Series 2B with a new flight deck. A total of 380 748s were built, with production ending in 1987. Of these, 89 were built in India by Hindustan Aeronautics Ltd. The Advanced Turbo Prop (ATP) was BAe's follow-on aircraft to its 748. It seats 60-72 passengers and features new engines and avionics. ATP development began in March 1984 and it entered service in April 1986. From the start, the type was plagued by technical problems. In October 1992 BAe transferred the ATP to its Jetstream division, and the aircraft

Specifications (ATP)

Powerplant
Two Pratt & Whitney Canada PW127D turboprops, each rated at 1,781 kW (2,388 shp) maximum continuous power

Dimensions
Length: 26 m (85 ft 4 in)
Height: 7.59 m (24 ft 11 in)
Wing span: 30.63 m (100 ft 6 in)

Weights
Empty operating: 14,242 kg (31,400 lb)
MTOW: 23,678 kg (52,200 lb)

Performance
Cruise speed: 437 km/h (236 kts)
Range: 1,741 km (939 nm)

British Aerospace 748 & ATP/Jetstream 61 (UK)

was redesignated Jetstream 61. The J61 name came with several upgrades but no orders were received. The ATP program ended in early 1995, when British Aerospace agreed to merge its regional aircraft products with the Aerospatiale/Alenia ATR team. As part of the deal, BAe agreed to cease production of the ATP. Just over 60 were built.

Variants

748: Low-wing pressurized twin-turboprop
ATP: Advanced turboprop regional airliner with PW126A engines
ATP/Jetstream 61: Advanced turboprop regional airliner, with modernized cabin and improved PW127D engine

Doomed from the beginning the ATP's production ended less than ten years from the time it entered service

Status
Production completed

Operators
Bazair, Airfast Indonesia PT, Bouraq Indonesia, Emerald Airways, Air Creebec, First Air, Merpati Nusantara Airlines, Air Europa Express, British Airways, British Regional Airlines, Manx Airlines, Untied Feeder Service

The first 748 was designed in the late-1950s

British Aerospace Jetstream 31/41 (UK)

Passengers: 29

Development/History

The Jetstream 31 is a 19-seat twin turboprop pressurized regional airliner built by British Aerospace. The Jetstream 41 is its stretched sibling, which accommodates 27-29 passengers. The J31 design began as the Handley Page Jetstream 1. This first flew in August 1967, with first deliveries in June 1969. Handley Page built about 26 for military applications. In 1978 successor company BAe decided to develop the design, and a modified Jetstream 1 flew in March 1980. Deliveries began in December 1982. In 1988 production switched to the Super 31, or J32. The J32 features and upgraded interior, increased take-off weight, and uprated engines. BAe has built over 380 J31/32s, and over 360 of these are still in service. Over 300 J31s are being leased by BAe's Jetstream leasing company, JSX. BAe first revealed the J41 in 1988. Launched in May 1989, the J41 first flew in September 1991, with first deliveries in November 1992. Production of the J41 ended in 1997, with deliveries of the J31/32 ending two years earlier.

Specifications (J41)

Powerplant
Two AlliedSignal/Garrett TPE331-14GR/HR turboprops, each rated at 1,230 kW (1,650 shp)

Dimensions
Length: 19.25 m (63 ft 2 in)
Height: 5.74 m (18 ft 10 in)
Wing span: 18.29 m (60 ft 0 in)

Weights
Empty operating: 6,416 kg (14,144 lb)
MTOW: 10,886 kg (24,000 lb)

Performance
Cruise speed: 547 km/h (295 kts)
Range: 1,433 km (774 nm)

Variants
J31: Twin-turboprop regional airliner
J41: Twin-turboprop regional airliner with payload/range and performance improvements

Status
Production completed

Operators
Eastern Australia Airlines, J-Air, Origin Pacific Airways, Flying Enterprise, Regional Airlines, Sun-Air of Scandinavia, Atlantic Coast Airlines, CCAir, Chautauqua Airlines, Express Airlines, Trans States Airlines, WestAir Commuter Airlines

Pan Am was the original, now defunct, J41 launch customer

Production of J41 lasted only 6 years

Canadair Regional Jet (Canada)

Passengers: 50

Development/History

Canadair's Regional Jet (RJ) is the first of its kind: a 50-seat transport designed for long, thin regional routes. It is derived from the company's Challenger business jet (see), and uses the same General Electric CF34 turbofans. Seating is four abreast. The RJ program was launched in March 1989, and the aircraft first flew in May 1991. Canadian certification was awarded in July 1992, followed by US FAA and European JAA certification in January 1993. The RJ is replacing both turboprop transports and ageing small jets, such as the DC-9 and Fokker 28. The CRJ-X will seat 70 passengers, and use improved versions of the CF34.

Variants

RJ200: Twin-turbofan regional transport seating 50 passengers over 985 nm range
RJ200ER: Extended Range version capability with optional increase in maximum T-O weight to 23,133 kg and optional fuel capacity, for range of 1,645 nm
CRJ 700A: Stretched version seating 70

Specifications (RJ100)

Powerplant
Two General Electric CF34-3A1 turbofans, each rated at 41.01 kN (9,220 lbst) with APR (automatic power reserve)

Dimensions
Length: 26.77 m (87 ft 10 in)
Height: 6.22 m (20 ft 5 in)
Wing span: 21.21 m (69 ft 7 in)

Weights
Empty operating: 13,653 kg (30,100 lb)
MTOW: 21,523 kg (47,450 lb)

Performance
Cruise speed: 786 km/h (424 kts)
Range: 1,816 km (980 nm)

Canadair Regional Jet (Canada)

Status
In production

Operators
SA Express, China United Airlines, Air Littoral, Brit Air, Lauda Air, Lufthansa CityLine, Tyrolean Airways, Air Canada, AMR Eagle, Atlantic Southeast Airlines, Comair, SkyWest Airlines

The first of its kind, Canadair's Regional Jet replaces both turboprops and small jets

The CRJ uses the same GE CF34 turbofan engines as its sister craft, the Challenger business jet

De Havilland Canada DHC (Dash) 7 (Canada)

Passengers: 50-54

Development/History

A four-engine transport, the Dash 7 has
enough installed engine power to operate from
Short Take-Off and Landing (STOL) runways
only 685 m (2,160 ft) in length. The Dash 7 can
seat up to 54 passengers, or cargo, or a mix.
The Dash 7 program began in 1972, and the
type made its first flight in March 1975.
Canadian certification was awarded in May
1977. First production version was the Series
100, followed by the heavier Series 150. Cargo
versions of both were the Series 101 and 151,
respectively. DHC proposed further versions,
including the Series 300, a 70-seat stretch.
These were cancelled, partly due to the advent
of twin engine transports with the same
capacity, such as the ATR 72. DHC built 111
Dash 7s, with production ending in the late
1980s. Most of these are still in service.

Specifications (DHC-7 Series 100)

Powerplant
Four Pratt & Whitney Canada PT6A-50 turboprops, each flat-rated at 835
kW (1,120 shp) for take-off

Dimensions
Length: 24.54 m (80 ft 6 in)
Height: 7.98 m (26 ft 2 in)
Wing span: 28.35 m (93 ft)

Weights
Empty operating: 12,560 kg (27,690 lb)
MTOW: 19,958 kg (44,000 lb)

Performance
Cruise speed: 399 km/h (215 kts)
Range: 2,168 km (1,170 nm)

Variants

Series 100: Four-engine transport
Series 150: Heavier version
Series 101: Cargo version of Series 100
Series 151: Cargo version of Series 150

Status

Production completed

Operators

National Aviation Company, Arkia, Pelita Air Services, Greenlandair, LTA, Paradise Island Airlines, Piedmont Airlines, Voyageur Airways

De Havilland Canada built 111 Dash 7s, most of which are still in service

De Havilland Canada DHC (Dash) 8 (Canada)

Passengers: 30-36

Development/History

The Dash 8 is the latest in a long line of DHC's Canadian-built turboprop transports. Unlike the Dash 5, 6, and 7, however, the Dash 8 is built for regional airline operations from normal airports. A high-wing, pressurized, twin-engine design, the Dash 8 comes in two basic versions, the 30-36 seat Dash 8-100 and the stretched 50-56 seat Dash 8-300. Originally known as the Dash X, the Dash 8 program began in 1978. The Dash 8-100 entered service in December 1984. DHC also offers the Dash 8-200, a faster -100 with greater commonality with the -300. The -300 was first announced in mid 1985. It entered service in March 1989. It uses uprated PW123B engines. DHC has built over 300 -100s and over 100 -300s. Production is continuing. DHC also proposed the Dash 8-400, a further stretch version with new engines. It will carry 70 passengers at 648 km/h (350 kt) speeds. The -400 will be delivered in 1999.

Specifications (DHC-8-100)

Powerplant
Two Pratt & Whitney Canada PW120A turboprops, each rated at 1,491 kW (2,000 shp) with automatic power reserve

Dimensions
Length: 22.25 m (73 ft)
Height: 7.49 m (24 ft 7 in)
Wing span: 25.91 m (85 ft)

Weights
Empty operating: 10,251 kg (22,600 lb)
MTOW: 15,650 kg (34,500 lb)

Performance
Cruise speed: 439 km/h (237 kts)
Range: 1,519 km (820 nm)

Variants

DHC-8-100: Turboprop transport with choice of PW120A or PW121 engines
DHC-8-300: Stretched version with extended wingtips, 3.43 m two-lug fuselage extension giving standard seating for 50 at cm pitch or 56 at 74 cm pitch
DHC-8-400: Further stretched version seating 72-78 passengers

Status

In production

The Dash 8-200 in desert training

De Havilland Canada DHC (Dash) 8 (Canada)

Operators
SA Express, Ansett New Zealand, Eastern Australia Airlines, Great China Airlines, Sunstate Airlines, Brymon Airways, Tyrolean Airways, Wideroe's Flyveselskap, Air Alliance, Air BC, Air Nova, Air Ontario, Allegheny Airlines, Canadian Regional Airlines, Horizon Air, LIAT, Mesaba Airlines, Piedmont Airlines

A further stretched version seating up to 78 passengers

A Dash 8 taxiing on the runway

Dornier 328 (Germany)

Passengers: 30-33

Development/History

Dornier's 328 is a twin turboprop 30-33 seat pressurized regional airliner. Capable of 620 km/h (335 kt) speeds, the 328 is the fastest plane in its class. Dornier, now part of Daimler Benz Aerospace, began research on a new 30-seat plane in 1984. The 328 project was launched and the design frozen in mid 1989. A 328 prototype flew in late 1991, but flight tests were stopped to re-engine the plane with more powerful PW119Bs. Later that year a 328 prototype suffered a near-catastrophic propeller failure. Still, Dornier pushed on. JAA certification came in October 1993, followed by first delivery. The 328 is built by an international team of subcontractors. The fuselage is built by South Korea's Daewoo and Italy's Aermacchi. Israel Aircraft Industries builds the wings. Britain's Westland builds the engine nacelles and fuselage doors. The engines, of course, come from Pratt & Whitney Canada.

Specifications (Do 328)

Powerplant
Two Pratt & Whitney Canada PW119B turboprops, each rated at 1,380 kW (1,850 shp) for normal take-off

Dimensions
Length: 21.22 m (69 ft 8 in)
Height: 7.24 m (23 ft 9 in)
Wing span: 20.98 m (68 ft 10 in)

Weights
Empty operating: 8,175 kg (18,022 lb)
MTOW: 13,640 kg (30,071 lb)

Performance
Cruise speed: 620 km/h (335 kts)
Range: 1,556 km (840 nm)

Variants

Do 328: Twin-turboprop pressurized regional airliner seating 30-33 passengers
Do 328JET: Turbofan version of Do 328 with seating for 32-34 passengers at 79 cm pitch

Status

In production

Operators

Afrimex Aviation, Formosa Airlines, Air Engiadina, Minerva Italy, Horizon Air, Lone Star Airlines, Mountain Air Express, PSA Airlines, SATENA, Proteus Air System, Aspen Mountain Air

The Do 328 turboprop is a regional airliner built by an international cast of characters

Dornier 328 _(Germany)

The Do 328JET moved the aircraft into the turbofan market

Embraer EMB-120 Brasilia (Brazil)

Passengers: 30

Development/History

The EMB-120 Brasilia is a 30-seat twin turboprop regional airliner built by Brazil's Embraer. A low-wing pressurized design with retractable landing gear and digital avionics, the Brasilia competes with the DHC Dash 8-100, BAe's Jetstream 41, and the Saab 340. The EMB-120 program began in the early 1980s. A prototype flew in July 1983. Brazil's CTA certified the EMB-120 in May 1985, and the type entered service in August 1985. In late 1986 Embraer introduced a hot-and-high variant, with uprated PW118A engines. Embraer also builds the EMB-120QC, a convertible passenger/cargo aircraft, and the EMB-120ER (Enhanced Range). Finally, in 1994 Embraer introduced the EMB-120ER Advanced, with quieter propellers, an improved interior, and other upgrades. As of late 1997 Embraer had built almost 330 Brasilias, and production is continuing.

Specifications (EMB-120ER)

Powerplant
Two Pratt & Whitney Canada PW118 turboprops, each rated at 1,342 kW (1,800 shp)

Dimensions
Length: 20.07 m (65 ft 10.75 in)
Height: 6.35 m (20 ft 10 in)
Wing span: 19.78 m (64 ft 10.75 in)

Weights
Empty operating: 7,150 kg (15,763 lb)
MTOW: 11,990 kg (26,433 lb)

Performance
Cruise speed: 555 km/h (300 kts)
Range: 1,575 km (850 nm)

Embraer EMB-120 Brasilia (Brazil)

The Brazilian EMB-120's principal customer group has been North American regional airlines

Variants
EMB-120ER: Twin-turboprop passenger and cargo transport, extended range and increased maximum T-O weight

Status
In production

Operators
Flight West Airlines, Delta Air Transport, Flandre Air, Atlantic Southeast Airlines, Comair, Continental Airlines, FloridaGulf Airlines, Great Lakes Aviation, Mountain West Airlines, Rio Sul, SkyWest Airlines, WestAir Commuter Airlines

The Brasilia is also available in a cargo variant

Embraer EMB-120 Brasilia (Brazil)

The EMB-120 Brasilia's sleek appearance is enhanced by the low-wing design and retractable landing gear

ERJ-145 Amazon (Brazil)

Passengers: 50 (one class)

Development/History

The ERJ-145 Amazon is a 48-seat twinjet regional aircraft built by Brazil's Embraer. The new aircraft is a stretched ERJ-120 with new wings and engines. The original ERJ-145 design used the ERJ-120's straight wings with turbofans mounted above the wings. In March 1991, Embraer changed the design to include new swept wings with engines mounted beneath the wings. In December 1991 Embraer approved a second redesign of the ERJ-145, with engines on the rear fuselage. In June 1993, Embraer gave a go-ahead to the Amazon project. A prototype was rolled out and flown in August 1995, over two years later than originally planned. Embraer delivered the first ERJ-145s in March 1997. As of early 1998 Embraer had 228 orders and 318 options for the ERJ-145.

Variants

ERJ-145: Twin-turbofan regional airliner seating 50 passengers

Specifications (ERJ-145)

Powerplant
Two Allison AE 3007A turbofans, each rated at 31.32 kN (7,040 lbst)

Dimensions
Length: 27.93 m (91 ft 7.5 in)
Height: 6.71 m (22 ft 0.25 in)
Wing span: 20.04 m (65 ft 9 in)

Weights
Empty operating: 11,585 kg (25,540 lb)
MTOW: 19,200 kg (42,329 lb)

Performance
Cruise speed: 760 km/h (410 kts)
Range: 1,482 km (800 nm)

ERJ-145 Amazon (Brazil)

Status
In production

Operators
Flight West Airlines, British Regional Airlines, Regional Airlines, AMR Eagle, Continental Express, Pena Transportes Aeroe (PENTA), Rio Sul

The ERJ-145 uses a stretched EMB-120 fuselage, seating up to twenty more passengers

The Amazon prototype was delivered more than two years behind schedule

ERJ-145 Amazon (Brazil)

Despite delays, the ERJ-145 has played surprisingly well in the regional aircraft market

Fokker 28 (Netherlands)

Passengers: 85

Development/History

The F28 Friendship is a twin engine narrow-body jetliner built by Fokker of the Netherlands. A 65-85 seat short/medium range design, the F28 competed with Douglas's DC-9 and BAC's 1-11. The F28 uses Rolls-Royce Spey engines mounted on the rear fuselage. The F28 program began in the early 1960s, with the first prototype flying in May 1967. The first F28 was the Mk 1000, a 65-seat model. It was available with a side-loading freight door for combined passenger/cargo operations as the Mk 1000-C. The Mk 1000 was followed by the stretched 79-seat Mk 2000, which first flew in April 1971. The short Mk 3000 and long (85-seat) Mk 4000 featured greater wing span and improved engines. The Mk 4000 was the final variant. Fokker built 241 F28s. Production ended in late 1986, but Fokker went on to build the derivative F100.

Specifications (F28 Mk 4000)

Powerplant
Two Rolls-Royce RB183-2 Mk 555-15P turbofans, each rated at 44 kN (9,900 lbst)

Dimensions
Length: 26.76 m (87 ft 9.5 in)
Height: 8.47 m (27 ft 9.5 in)
Wing span: 25.07 m (82 ft 3 in)

Weights
Empty operating: 17,645 kg (38,900 lb)
MTOW: 33,110 kg (73,000 lb)

Performance
Cruise speed: 678 km/h (366 kts)
Range: 2,085 km (1,125 nm)

Fokker 28 (Netherlands)

The Fokker F28 was powered by Rolls-Royce Spey engines

Variants

F28 Mk 1000: Twin-engined narrow-body jetliner

F28 Mk 1000-C: Combined cargo/passenger version

F28 Mk 2000: Stretched version seating 79 passengers

F28 Mk 3000: Shortened version seating with greater wing span and improved engines

F28 Mk 4000: Stretched version seating 85 passengers with a greater wing span

Status

Production completed

Operators

Libyan Arab Airlines, Air Niugini, Ansett Australia, Ian Asseman Airlines, Merpati Nusantara Airlines, SAS, Canadair Regional Airlines, Horizon Air, US Airways

The Fokker 28 ended production roughly a decade before Fokker itself shut its doors

Fokker 50 (Netherlands)

Passengers: 50

Development/History

Fokker developed the F50 as a modernized follow-on to its F27. The F50 is about the same size as its forebear, but features new engines, avionics, and other systems. The Rolls-Royce Dart engines have been replaced with Pratt & Whitney Canada PW125Bs, and there is an electronic flight instrumentation system (EFIS). The F50 program began in November 1983, and an F50 first flew in December 1985. Fokker delivered 207 F50s by late 1997. The baseline F50 is known as the Series 100 and was also available as a high performance variant, with PW127B turboprops. Fokker also built the Fokker 60, a 58 seat stretch version ordered by the Netherlands Air Force. It featured a large cargo door on the starboard side of the fuselage. The F60 was to be delivered in May 1996 and was also offered as a civil passenger and freight aircraft. In early 1996 Fokker Aircraft collapsed after DASA halted financial support. The company declared bankruptcy and halted production of all aircraft.

Specifications (Fokker 50-100)

Powerplant
Two Pratt & Whitney Canada PW125B turboprops, each flat-rated at 1,864 kW (2,500 shp)

Dimensions
Length: 25.25 m (83 ft 10 in)
Height: 8.32 m (27 ft 4 in)
Wing span: 29 m (95 ft 2 in)

Weights
Empty operating: 12,520 kg (27,602 lb)
MTOW: 19,950 kg (43,980 lb)

Performance
Cruise speed: 522 km/h (282 kts)
Range: 2,253 km (1,216 nm)

Variants
Fokker 50-100: Follow-on to the F27 twin-turboprop pressurized high-wing transport
Fokker 60: Stretched version seating 58 passengers

Status
Production completed

Operators
Ethiopian Airlines, Formosa Airlines, Malaysia Airlines, Philippine Airlines, Skywest Airlines, Air Nostrum, Contact Air, KLM CityHopper, SAS Commuter, Skyways (Sweden), Rio Sul, TAM-Transportes Aereos Regionals SA

The Fokker 50 and 60 were derived from the Fokker 27

Fokker 100/70 (Netherlands)

Passengers: 107 (F100) and 70-78 (F70)

Development/History

The F100 is a 107-seat stretched follow-on to the Fokker 28 (see). The F100 features new Tay 650 engines and a digital 'glass' cockpit. F100 development began in 1983. The first F100 flew in November 1986, and Swissair received the first production F100 in February 1988. The F100 received a boost in March 1989, when American Airlines ordered 75 aircraft, the largest order in Fokker's history. The F100 is an international product. In addition to the Rolls-Royce engines, the wings came from Short Brothers in Northern Ireland. The fuselage was built by Daimler Benz Aerospace, which was Fokker's majority shareholder. In 1992, Fokker decided to revive the old F28 fuselage, with the F100's systems and Tay 620 engines. This became the Fokker 70, a 70-78 seat regional jet. Fokker launched the F70 in June 1993, and deliveries began in late 1994. Fokker built over 250 F100s. Fokker also built over 30 F70s. Production ended in April 1997.

Specifications (F100)

Powerplant
Two Rolls-Royce Tay Mk 620 turbofans, each rated at 61.6 kN (13,850 lbst)

Dimensions
Length: 35.53 m (116 ft 6.75 in)
Height: 8.51 m (27 ft 10.5 in)
Wing span: 28.08 m (92 ft 1.5 in)

Weights
Empty operating: 24,593 kg (54,217 lb)
MTOW: 43,090 kg (95,000 lb)

Performance
Maximum speed: 856 km/h (462 kts)
Range: 2,389 km (1,290 nm)

Fokker built over 50 F70s before production ended

Fokker 100/70 (Netherlands)

The F100 is a stretched version of the F28 twin-engine jetliner

Variants

F100: Stretched version of F28 twin-engined narrow-bodied jetliner

F70: 70-78 seat version twin-engined narrow-bodied jetliner

Status

Production completed

Operators

SilkAir, Vietnam Airlines, Austrian Airlines, KLM CityHopper, Air Ivoire, China Easter Airlines, Korean Air, Sempati Air, Air UK, Alpi Eagles, TAT European Airlines, American Airlines, Midway Airlines, TAM-Transportes Aereos Regionals SA, US Airways

The F70 revived the F28 fuselage

Ilyushin Il-96 (Russia)

Passengers: 300 (one class)

Development/History

The Il-96 is a four-engine wide-body commercial jet transport. Designed as a follow-on to the Il-86, the Il-96 can be distinguished from its predecessor by larger engines and winglets. The Il-96 is slightly shorter, and seats 300. Like the Il-86, the Il-96 resembles the Airbus A340. Il-96 design work began in the mid-1980s. The first of five prototypes flew in September 1988. The baseline version, the Il-96-300, began service in late 1992. Due to financial problems, only a handful of Il-96s have been built at the Voronezh production line. Il-96-300s have been delivered to Aeroflot Russian International Airlines (ARIA), and Domodedovo Air Lines. While the Il-96-300's Perm PS-90 engines are a major improvement over the Il-86's NK-86s, Ilyushin is co-operating with American manufacturers to 'Westernize' the plane. The Il-96M variant uses Pratt & Whitney PW2337 turbofans and Rockwell-Collins avionics. It has greater range than the Il-96-300, and features a two-crew flight deck. There is also a freighter variant, the Il-96MT.

Specifications (Il-96-300)

Powerplant
Four Perm/Soloviev PS-90A turbofans, each rated at 156.9 kN (35,275 lbst)

Dimensions
Length: 55.35 m (181 ft 7.25 in);
Height: 17.57 m (57 ft 7.75 in);
Wing span: 57.66 m (189 ft 2 in)

Weights
Empty operating: 117,000 kg (257,940 lb);
MTOW: 216,000 kg (476,200 lb)

Performance
Cruise speed: 850 km/h (459 kts);
Range: 7,500 km (4,050 nm)

The first Il-96M, a modified Il-96-300, flew in April 1993. Il-96M/MT orders have arrived from ARIA and Partnairs, a Dutch leasing company. In May 1997 the first Il-96T, the Westernized freighter, made its first flight. Russian certification came in late 1997.

Variants

Il-96-300: Four-turbofan wide-bodied triplex fly-by-wire transport seating 300 passengers

Il-96M: Stretched passenger or freight version, powered by four Pratt & Whitney PW2337 engines and western avionics (Collins digital EFIS with DO-178A standard software)

Il-96T: Westernized freighter version with 4.85m x 2.87m cargo door forward of wing on port side capable of handling nearly double the maximum payload of the Il-96M (58,000kg)

Status

In production

Operators

Aeroflot Russian International Airlines, Domodedovo Airlines, Russia State Transport Company

The IL-96 is hampered by financial problems

The IL-96M has western avionics

Lockheed Martin L-1011 TriStar (USA)

Passengers: 246 (two class)

Development/History

The L-1011 TriStar, a three-engine medium-capacity, medium-range wide-body, was Lockheed's only jetliner program. It arrived on the market the same time as its direct competitor, Douglas's DC-10. The TriStar's development was incredibly painful, resulting in engine manufacturer Rolls-Royce going into bankruptcy due to problems with its all-new high-bypass RB.211 turbofan. The first L-1011 flew in November 1970, nearly five years after Lockheed began design work. The first model, the L-1011-1, was delivered to Eastern Air Lines in April 1972. It was followed by the L-1011-100, -200, -250, and -500, with increasingly long ranges. The -500 fuselage is shortened by 4.1 m (13 ft 6 in). The L-1011 was very advanced for its time. It included such innovations as four independent hydraulic control systems, and avionics for an all-weather landing capability. A total of 250 L-1011s were built, with production ending in 1984.

Specifications (L-1011-500)

Powerplant
Three Rolls-Royce RB.211-524B4 turbofans, each rated at 222.4 kN (50,000 lbst)

Dimensions
Length: 50.05 m (164 ft 3 in)
Height: 16.87 m (55 ft 4 in)
Wing span: 47.34 m (155 ft 4 in)

Weights
Empty operating: 108,925 kg (240,139 lb)
MTOW: 224,980 kg (496,000 lb)

Performance
Cruise speed: 895 km/h (483 kts)
Range: 9,815 km (5,297 nm)

Lockheed Martin L-1011 TriStar (USA)

Variants
L-1011-1: Three-engine medium-capacity, medium-range wide-body airliner
L-1011-100, -200, -250, -500: Increasingly longer-range versions; -500 has shortened fuselage by 4.1 m and range of 5,297 nm

Status
Production completed

Operators
Safair, Air China, HeavyLift Cargo Airlines, Southern Air Transport, Gulf Air, Saudi Arabian Airlines, Caledonian Airways, TAP-Air Portugal, Air Transat, American Trans Air, Delta Air Lines, Rich International Airways, Trans World Airlines

Orbital Sciences uses an L-1011 to launch the Pegasus Upper Stage vehicle

McDonnell Douglas DC-8 (USA)

Passengers: 259 or 29,257 kg payload

Development/History

The DC-8 was Douglas's, then McDonnell Douglas's answer to the Boeing 707. A four-engine medium/long-range aircraft, the DC-8 program was launched in June 1955. Pan Am launched the type, and a prototype flew in May 1958. The first version, the Series 10, was FAA certified in August 1959 and entered service in September. The Series 10 was used on domestic routes, but it was followed in 1960 by the Series 30, an intercontinental version. Final versions were Super 61, 62, and 63, long-range, high-capacity versions which all entered service in 1967. Douglas built 556 DC-8s by the time production ended in May 1972. Most DC-8s were built with Pratt & Whitney JT3D engines, as on the 707. Early DC-8s had the Pratt JT4A or JT3C, while the Series 40 offered the Rolls-Royce Conway. In the early 1980s 110 Super 61s, 62s and 63s were re-engined with CFM56 engines, becoming Super 71s, 72s, and 73s. Most Super 70 series DC-8s are still in service, along with 50-70 other DC-8s.

Specifications (DC-8 Series 73)

Powerplant
Four CFM International (General Electric/SNECMA) CFM56-2-C1 turbofans, each rated at 97.9 kN (22,000 lbst)

Dimensions
Length: 57.12 m (187 ft 5 in)
Height: 12.92 m (42 ft 5 in)
Wing span: 45.23 m (148 ft 5 in)

Weights
Empty operating: 75,500 kg (166,500 lb)
MTOW: 161,025 kg (355,000 lb)

Performance
Cruise speed: 850 km/h (459 kts)
Range: 8,950 km (4,830 nm)

McDonnell Douglas DC-8 (USA)

The DC-8 program was launched in 1955

Variants
Series 10: Four-engined medium/long-range transport
Series 30: Intercontinental version
Super 61, 62 and 63: Long-range high-capacity versions
Super 71, 72 and 73: Re-engined mixed cargo/passenger versions

Status
Production completed

Operators
MK Airlines, Ansett Air Freight, Air Transport International, Airborne Express, American International Airways, Arrow Air, DHL Airways, Emery Worldwide Airlines, Fine Air, United Parcel Service

The DC-8 was McDonnell's first jet transport

McDonnell Douglas DC-9 (USA)

Passengers: 105-115

Development/History

The DC-9 program began in the 1950s, as a Douglas proposal for a short/medium range 75-seat narrow-body jetliner to complement the long-range DC-8. Douglas launched the DC-9 program in April 1963. The first DC-9 was the Series 10, a 90-seat design which received FAA certification in November 1965 and entered service in December. This was followed by the extended-wing Series 20, the 119-seat Series 30, and the 125-seat Series 40. There were also freight and convertible freight/passenger variants, and a military cargo variant, which the US Air Force designated the C-9. The final version of the DC-9 was the stretched 139-seat Series 50, which entered service in August 1975. DC-9 production ended in the early 1980s, but Douglas began building DC-9 Super 80, or MD-80. A total of 976 DC-9s were built, including 43 C-9s. The majority of these remain in service, with most major US airlines and quite a few others.

Specifications (DC-9 Series 30)

Powerplant
Two Pratt & Whitney JT8D-9s, each rated at 64.5 kN (14,500 lbst); also available with uprated JT8D-11, -15, -17

Dimensions
Length: 36.37 m (119 ft 4 in)
Height: 8.38 m (27 ft 6 in)
Wing span: 28.47 m (93 ft 5 in)

Weights
Empty operating: 25,940 kg (57,190 lb)
MTOW: 54,885 kg (121,000 lb)

Performance
Cruise speed: 907 km/h (490 kts)
Range: 3,095 km (1,670 nm)

The DC-9 was the short-range partner to the DC-8

McDonnell Douglas DC-9 (USA)

Variants
Series 10: Short/medium-range narrow-body jetliner
Series 20: Extended wing version
Series 30: 119 passenger capacity
Series 40: 125 passenger capacity
C-9: Military cargo variant
Series 50: Stretched version
Super 80 (which became the MD-80): Twin-turbofan short/medium-range airliner with maximum seating for 172 passengers

Status
Production completed

Operators
Aerocalifornia, Midwest Express, Northwest Airlines, USA Jet Airlines, SAS, Sun Air, Cebu Pacific Air, Aviaco, Aeromexico, Air Canada, Airborne Express, Continental Airlines, Trans World Airlines, ValuJet (n/k/a AirTran), Finnair, Hawaiian Air

A total of 976 DC-9s were built

The DC-9 was the first US airliner to feature rear-mounted engines

McDonnell Douglas (DC-10)

Passengers: 255-270 (mixed class), 380 (all-economy)

Development/History

The Douglas DC-10 is a three-engined medium/long-range wide-body jetliner with seating for 255-380 passengers. It made its first flight on August 29, 1970. FAA certification came in July 1971, and the DC-10 entered service in August. The first model was the DC-10 Series 10, designed for US domestic service and powered by General Electric CF6 engines. The CF6-powered Series 30 was the first intercontinental version and was also available as the Series 30ER (Extended Range). The Series 40, entering service in late 1972, used Pratt & Whitney JT9D engines. The DC-10 provided competition for the Lockheed's L-1011. The DC-10 program ended in 1989. Production totalled 446 aircraft. Of these, 60 were KC-10As.

Specifications (DC-10 Series 30)

Powerplant
Three General Electric CF6-50C turbofans, each rated at 227 kN (51,000 lbst)

Dimensions
Length: 55.5 m (182 ft 1 in)
Height: 17.7 m (58 ft 1 in)
Wing span: 50.4 m (165 ft 5 in)

Weights
Empty operating: 121,198 kg (267,197 lb)
MTOW: 259,450 kg (572,000 lb)

Performance
Cruise speed: 880 km/h (475 kts)
Range: 7,413 km (4,000 nm)

Early DC-10s had three GE CF6 engines, while Series 40 DC-10s were equipped with JT9D engines

The DC-10 on display

Variants

Series 10: Three-engined medium/long-range wide-bodied airliner for domestic service
Series 10CF: Convertible freighter version
Series 30: Intercontinental version
Series 30F: Freighter version
Series 30CF: Convertible freighter version
Series 40: Powered by P&W JT9D engines; non-stop range of 5,800 miles

Status

Production completed

Operators

Ghana Airways, Nigeria Airways, Garuda Indonesia, Japan Airlines, AOM French Airlines, American Airlines, Continental Airlines, FedEx, Hawaiian Air, Northwest Airlines, United Airlines, Varig

The DC-10 came in both domestic and intercontinental variants

Raytheon 1900 (USA)

Passengers: 19

Development/History

The 1900 is a 19-seat pressurized twin turboprop built by Raytheon's Beech unit. Beech began 1900 development in 1979, as a follow-on to the Beechcraft C99, a 15-seat transport which ended production in 1975. The 1900 first flew in September 1982 and entered service in February 1984. The 1900 airframe is based on the Super King Air 200. Most 1900s are used by regional carriers. It is also used as a business transport. Several air forces use the type for transport duties, and US Air National Guard has designated them C-12J for electronic surveillance missions. Beech built 255 1900s (mostly 1900Cs) before switching to the current production model, the longer-ranged 1900D. It entered service in late 1991 and is externally distinguished by winglets. It also has a 'wet' wing (with integral fuel tanks instead of bladders) and an electronic flight instrumentation system (EFIS). Most important, the 1900D centre ceiling is 35.6 cm (14 in) higher than earlier 1900s, so you can stand up inside the cabin without banging your head.

Specifications (1900D)

Powerplant
Two Pratt & Whitney Canada PT6A-67D turboprops, each flat-rated at 954 kW (1,279 shp)

Dimensions
Length: 17.63 m (57 ft 10 in)
Height: 4.57 m (15 ft)
Wing span: 17.67 m (57 ft 12 in)

Weights
Empty operating: 4,785 kg (10,550 lb)
MTOW: 7,688 kg (16,950 lb)

Performance
Cruise speed: 533 km/h (288 kts)
Range: 2,776 km (1,498 nm)

Variants

1900C: Pressurized twin-turboprop regional transport
1900D: Longer-range version; range with 10 passengers, at long-range cruise power, with allowances for starting, taxi, T-O, climb and descent is 1,476 nm

Status

In production

Operators

Regional Air Lines, Falcon Express Cargo Airlines, Impulse Airlines, Air Littoral, Flandre Air, Proteus Air System, Air Alliance, Air Midwest, ALTA, Ameriflight, Central Mountain Air, Commutair, Continental Express, FloridaGulf Airlines, GP Express Airlines, Gulfstream International Airlines, Mesa Airlines, Mountain West Airlines, Skyway Airlines

The 1900C's airframe is based on the Super King Air 200

The 1900D is distinguished by both winglets and an additional 14 inches (356 cm) headroom

Saab 340 (Sweden)

Passengers: 35

Development/History

The 340 is a 30-37 seat regional airliner. Built by Sweden's Saab, the 340 was originally designed with Fairchild Industries as the SF 340A. Fairchild left the joint venture in 1985, and the SF 340 became the Saab 340. The program began in 1980, and a prototype first flew in January 1983. The 340 entered service in June 1984. The 340B is the current production model. It first flew in April 1989 and features uprated CT7 engines and improved range and payload. A twin-turboprop pressurized design, the 340 is available in cargo and executive variants. Saab proposed a stretched variant, and this became the nucleus of the Saab 2000. The 340 recently found a new role as a radar-equipped airborne early warning platform. This 340AEW is recognizable by the large rectangular Erieye radar carried above the fuselage. As of late 1995 Saab has built over 350 340s, mostly for European and North American operators. The 340 competes with the Do.328, EMB-120, Jetstream 41, and DHC-8-100. Production is continuing, and Saab is planning upgrades necessary to keep the 340 competitive into the next century.

Specifications (340B)

Powerplant
Two General Electric CT7-9B turboprops, each rated at 1,305 kW (1,750 shp) for take-off

Dimensions
Length: 19.73 m (64 ft 9 in)
Height: 6.97 m (22 ft 11 in)
Wing span: 21.44 m (70 ft 4 in)

Weights
Empty operating: 8,140 kg (17,945 lb)
MTOW: 13,155 kg (29,000 lb)

Performance
Cruise speed: 467 km/h (252 kts)
Range: 1,732 km (935 nm)

Saab 340 (Sweden)

The Saab 340 is operated by, primarily, European and North American customers

Variants

340A: Twin-turboprop regional and business transport
340B: Twin-turboprop regional and business transport, improved payload/range
340AEW: Airborne Early Warning version

Status

340A production completed
340B/B+/C in production

Operators

Air Nelson, Japan Air Commuter, Kendell Airlines, Crossair, KLM CityHopper, Skyways (Sweden), Business Express, Express Airlines, Flagship Airlines, Mesaba Airlines, Simmons Airlines, Wings West Airlines

The 340 found a new role as a radar-equipped airborne early warning platform

The Saab 340 also comes as an executive/corporate aircraft

Saab 2000 (Sweden)

Passengers: 50

Development/History

A twin-turboprop regional transport, the Saab 2000 is derived from the Saab 340. The 2000 has a longer fuselage, seating 50-58 passengers, and 33% larger wings than the 340. It also has larger Allison AE2100 engines, giving the 2000 superior range and speed. Thin and sleek, the 2000 is also a head-turner. It features six-bladed slow-revving swept propellers. The passenger doors are compatible with standard jetways. Saab began the 2000 program in December 1988. The first of three test aircraft flew in March 1992. The Saab 2000 received European JAA certification in March 1994, and US FAA certification one month later. Switzerland's Crossair received the first of 20 Saab 2000s in August 1994.

Variants

2000: Twin-turboprop regional transport seating 50 passengers
2000AEW&C: Projected airborne early warning and control variant employing spine-mounted Erieye radar

Specifications (Saab 2000)

Powerplant
Two Allison AE 2100A turboprops, each rated at 3,076 kW (4,125 shp)

Dimensions
Length: 27.03 m (88 ft 8.25 in)
Height: 7.73 m (25 ft 4 in)
Wing span: 24.76 m (81 ft 2.75 in)

Weights
Empty operating: 13,500 kg (29,762 lb)
MTOW: 22,000 kg (48,500 lb)

Performance
Cruise speed: 653 km/h (353 kts)
Range: 2,324 km (1,255 nm)

Saab 2000 (Sweden)

Status
In production

Operators
Air Marshall Islands,
Crossair, Med Airlines,
Regional Airlines, SAS
Commuter, Tatra Air

The Saab 2000 was developed as a stretched version of the 340

The Saab 2000 has both JAA and FAA certification

Shorts 330/360 (UK)

Passengers: 36

Development/History

The last aircraft designed and built by Short Brothers of Northern Ireland, the 330 and 360 are unpressurized twin turboprop passenger and utility aircraft. Both of the boxy, high-wing designs are powered by Pratt Canada PT6As. The 330 seats 30 passengers while the 360 seats 36. The 330 program began in the early 1970s as a derivative of the Shorts Skyvan utility aircraft. The first version, the 330-200, entered service in August 1976. The 360, a stretched 330-200, first flew in June 1981 and entered service in December 1982. Shorts considered plans to stretch the 360 into the 450, but these were dropped. Most 330s were bought by military users. The 360 was popular with commuter operators, until the current generation of pressurized turboprops (DHC-8-100, Saab 340, ATR 42, etc.) arrived in the mid 1980s. The US military is buying some used 360s for conversion to C-23s. The 330 ended production in 1989, while the 360 lingered on until 1991. Production totalled 179 330s and 164 360s. Most of these are still in service, and Shorts continues to support them.

Specifications (360F)

Powerplant
Two Pratt & Whitney Canada PT6A-67R turboprops, each rated at 1,062 kW (1,424 shp)

Dimensions
Length: 21.58 m (70 ft 9.5 in)
Height: 7.27 m (23 ft 10.25 in); wing span 22.8 m (74 ft 9.5 in)

Weights
Empty operating: 7,870 kg (17,350 lb)
MTOW: 12,292 kg (27,100 lb)

Performance
Cruise speed: 400 km/h (216 kts)
Range: 1,178 km (636 nm)

Variants

330-200: Unpressurized twin-turboprop passenger and utility aircraft seating 30 passengers
360: Stretched version seating 36 passengers

Status

Production completed

Operators

SAFT, Airnorth, Gill Airways, Streamline Aviation, Air Cargo Carriers, Airkenya, Pacific Island Aviation, Sunstate Airlines, BAC Express Airlines, British Regional Airlines, Executive Airlines

The Shorts 360 was the last aircraft built by Short Brothers of Northern Ireland

The 360's primary customer is the civilian commuter

Tupolev Tu-204 (Russia)

Passengers: 196 (two class)

Development/History

The Tu-204 is a narrow-body twinjet commercial transport designed by the Tupolev Design Bureau. Intended to replace the Tu-154, the Tu-204 seats 190-214 passengers and is about the same size as the Boeing 757 and Airbus A321. The Tu-204 program began in the early 1980s. The first of six prototypes flew in January 1989. Tu-204 cargo operations began in early 1993, and Russian passenger certification was awarded in early 1995. Small numbers of Tu-204s have been built at the Ulyanovsk production line. Full production, as with other CIS planes, is delayed pending the resolution of financial problems. The Tu-204 uses PS-90 engines and is available with Western engines and avionics. The Tu-204M uses Rolls-Royce RB.211-535 engines. The 204M, also known as the Tu-204-222, began flight tests in 1992. It is marketed by the British-Russian Aviation Company (BRAVIA).

Specifications (Tu-204)

Powerplant

Two Aviadvigatel PS-90A turbofans or two Rolls-Royce RB211 535 E4 turbofans.

Data below is for aircraft with PS-90As each rated at 158.3 kN (35,580 lbst)

Dimensions

Length: 46.0 m (150 ft 11 in)
Height: 13.90 m (45 ft 7.25 in)
Wing span: 42.0 m (137 ft 9.5 in)

Weights

Empty operating: 58,300 kg (128,530 lb)
MTOW: 94,600 kg (208,550 lb)

Performance

Cruise speed: 830 km/h (448 kts)
Range: 2,900 km (1,565 nm)

Tupolev Tu-204 (Russia)

The Tu-204's operators can choose between Russian engines or Rolls-Royce RB211 turbofans

Variants
Tu-204: Twin-turbofan medium-range airliner seating up to 214 passengers or maximum payload of 21,000 kg
Tu-204-220: Further increase in payload and T-O weight, small increase in fuel in wing centre-section and adjacent baggage hold
Tu-204-222: Same as 204-220 but with Collins Avionics

Status
In production

Operators
Aeroflot Russian International Airlines, Kras Air, Perm Airlines, Tupolev-Aerotrns, Tyumenaviatrans, Vnukovo Airlines

Unfortunately the Tu-204 will need more than love to come from Russia, as financial problems continue to plague the CIS manufacturers

Jane's Historic Military Aircraft Recognition Guide

From jet interceptors recently retired from military service to World War I bi-planes,
Jane's Historic Military Aircraft Recognition Guide is a complete directory of military aircraft preserved today

Also available in the Jane's series

Jane's Aircraft Recognition Guide

Jane's Aircraft Recognition Guide is the most comprehensive single volume on modern aviation.
Over 500 military and civil aircraft are included, providing unrivalled coverage of every major aircraft type flying today